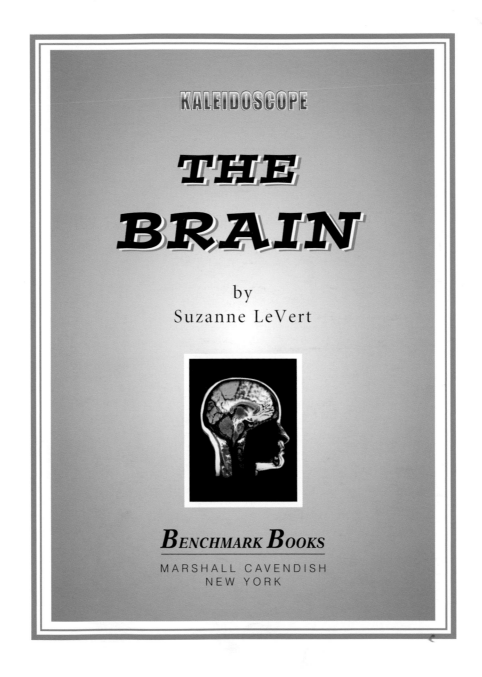

KALEIDOSCOPE

THE
BRAIN

by
Suzanne LeVert

BENCHMARK BOOKS

MARSHALL CAVENDISH
NEW YORK

Benchmark Books
Marshall Cavendish Corporation
99 White Plains Road
Tarrytown, NY 10591-9001
Website: www.marshallcavendish.com

Library of Congress Cataloging-in-Publication Data
LeVert, Suzanne.
The brain / by Suzanne LeVert.
   p.cm. – (Kaleidoscope)
Includes bibliographical references and index.
ISBN 0-7614-1308-1
1. Brain—Juvenile literature. [1. Brain.] I. Title. II. Series.
QP361.5 .L485 2001   612.8'2—dc21   00-050727

Photo Research by Anne Burns Images

Cover Photo by Scott Camazine, Photo Researchers, Inc.

The photographs in this book are used by permission and though the courtesy of: *Phototake:* Linda S. Nye, 5; Vladimir Pechanec, 22. *Photo Researchers Inc:* Bo Veisland, MI & I/Science Photo Library, 6; Pascall Goetgheluck/Science Photo Library, 9; Mehau Kulyk/Science Photo Library 10; Carlyn Iverson 13; John Bavosi/Photo Science Library, 17, 18, 39; Hattie Young/Science Photo Library 40. CNRI/Science Photo Library, 28; Alfred Psieka/Science Photo Library, 31; Will and Deni McIntyre, 36. *Peter Arnold:* Manfred Kage, 14; Alex Grey, 25; John Allison, 32, 33. *Photo Edit:* David Young Wolf, 21; Jeff Greenberg, 35; M. Ferguson, 43. *Omni Photo Communications:* Esbin/Anderson, 26.

Printed in Italy

6 5 4 3 2 1

CONTENTS

THOUGHT, EMOTION, MOVEMENT 4

THE BRAIN AND THE SPINAL CORD 7

YOU'VE GOT SOME NERVE 24

HOW NERVES WORK 29

WHEN THINGS GO WRONG 34

KEEP THINKING AND MOVING 42

GLOSSARY 44

FIND OUT MORE 46

INDEX 48

THOUGHT, EMOTION, MOVEMENT

Your brain is a remarkably complicated organ. It is where you feel emotions such as love and anger. It is where you think, decide, remember, and dream. Your brain also sends signals in the form of nerve impulses to every area in the body. These signals tell your body what to do, how to move, when and how to smile. In fact, your brain and the rest of your body are alive with billions of electrical and chemical signals that create the person you are and the activities you perform. Let's take a closer look at this amazing organ.

The human brain and nervous system regulate all body functions, including the beating of your heart, the way you smile, and what you feel and think.

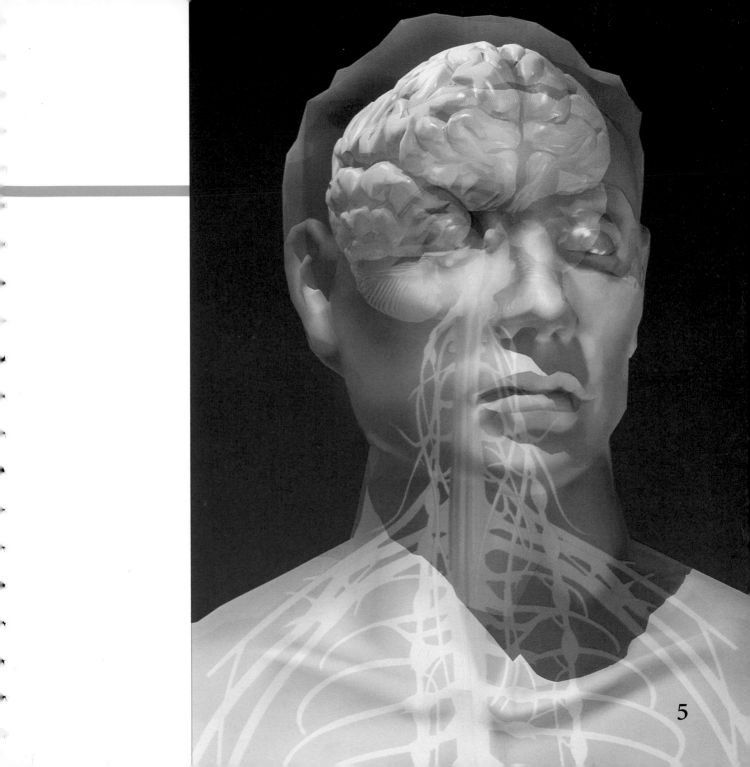

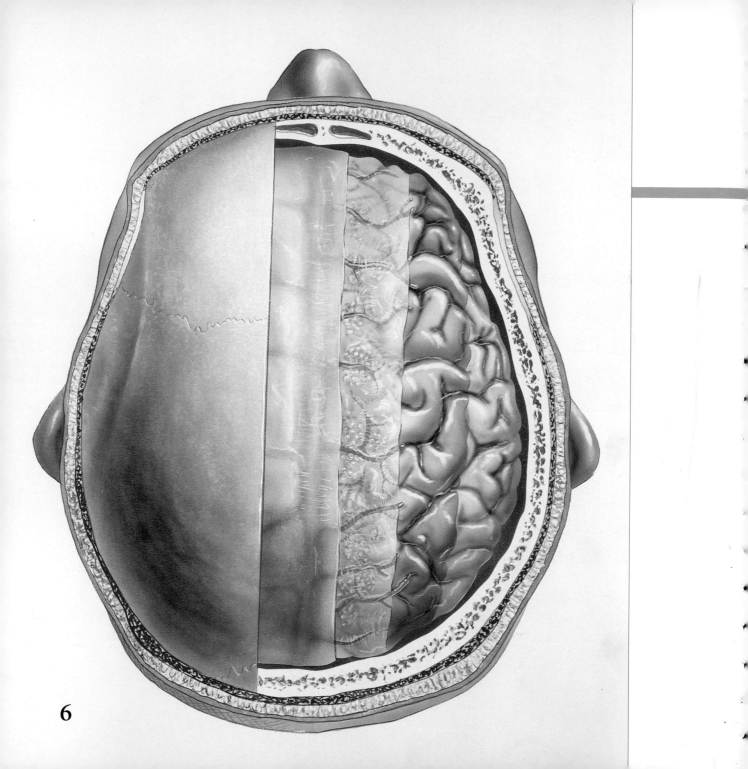

6

THE BRAIN AND THE SPINAL CORD

Your brain looks like a soft, pinkish gray sponge. It looks and feels a little like stiff gelatin and is wrinkled like a giant walnut. It rests inside your skull, which safely protects it from bumps and jolts. Three layers of *membranes* (thin sheets of body tissue) and a cushion of fluid give it extra protection. Your brain weighs less than three pounds and contains billions of individual nerve cells, also called *neurons*. Although it makes up only about 2 percent of an adult's body weight, it needs 20 percent of the body's blood and oxygen to nourish all of its cells and fuel its processes.

Your brain is protected by your skull, which is made up of twenty-two bones.

A network of blood vessels brings oxygen and blood sugar to brain cells. If you don't get enough oxygen or sugar, your brain can't function and you'll get dizzy and confused within just a minute or two. You might even faint. Then after only four to eight minutes without oxygen, your brain can become damaged. You could even die.

The brain has three main parts, the *cerebrum,* the *cerebellum,* the *brain stem,* and another area called the *limbic system.* All of them work together, but each has its own role to play.

The brain has three main parts: the cerebrum, the brain stem, and the cerebellum.

THE BRAIN

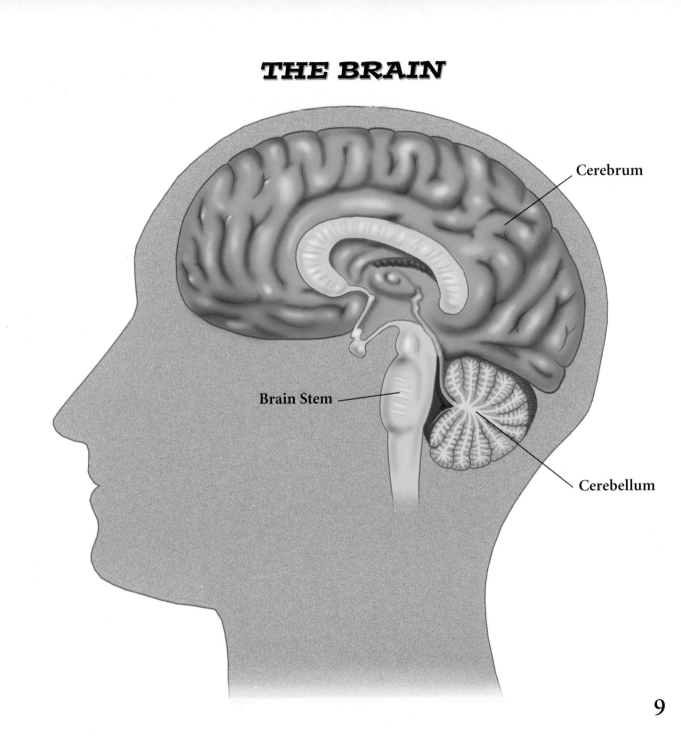

Cerebrum

Brain Stem

Cerebellum

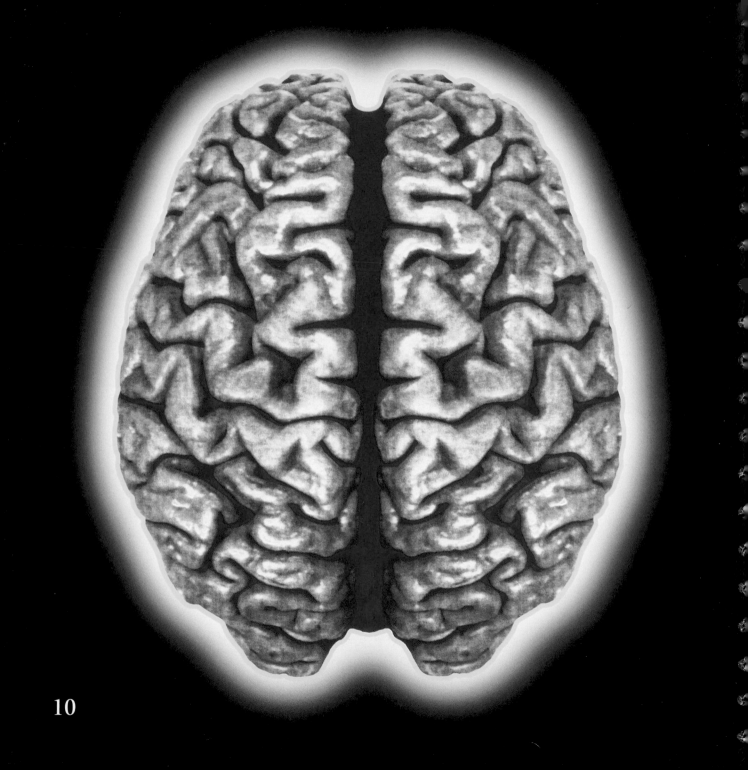

The Cerebrum

The cerebrum makes up seven tenths of your brain and it does most of your brain's work. It has a heavily folded surface. In fact, if you unfolded this covering, it would be almost three feet square. The pattern created by the folds is different in every human being. Your brain does most of its work here, including thinking, learning, decision making, joking, and moving.

The cerebrum is the largest part of the brain and is divided into two parts, called hemispheres.

The outer layer of the cerebrum, called the cortex, helps you move your *voluntary muscles*. Voluntary muscles are those that you can move just by thinking about it. If you want to turn a page of this book, for instance, one area of your cerebrum sends a signal to one small part of your cortex. The cortex then passes on the information to the motor area of the brain. A signal flashes down to the muscles in your hand and arm, telling them to turn the page. And all of this activity happens in less time than it takes for you to blink.

Whenever you raise your arm,
your brain sends a signal through
hundreds of thousands of nerve
cells to tell the muscles in your
arm to move.

13

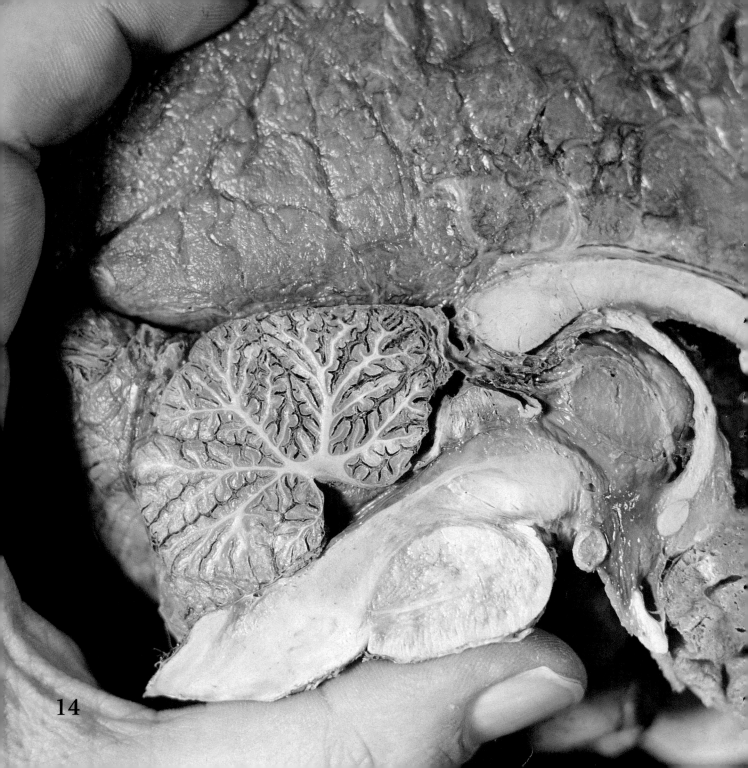

14

The Cerebellum

Located just below the cerebrum and behind the brain stem is the cerebellum. This part of the brain is only one eighth the size of the cerebellum, but it performs many essential tasks. The cerebellum's main job is to send messages to the muscles of the body about balance and precise movement. It makes sure your body muscles work together smoothly. It also helps your body "remember" how to move. The next time you walk down the stairs, notice that you don't have to figure out the distance between each step: you just go! That's your cerebellum at work.

The cerebellum helps your body move smoothly and precisely, and also helps control your balance and posture.

The Brain Stem

The brain stem helps maintain some of your body's automatic activities. It keeps your heartbeat steady, your breathing regular, and your digestion efficient without you even having to think about it. When you exercise, the brain stem tells your lungs to inhale more oxygen; if you become frightened, it tells your heart to beat faster and your muscles to tense, just in case you have to run away. The brain stem also triggers reflexes, such as sneezing and swallowing. Because these functions are vital to life, a blow to the back of the head can be deadly if it damages the brain stem.

The brain stem helps control involuntary, unconscious body functions, such as the heartbeat, breathing, and blood pressure.

16

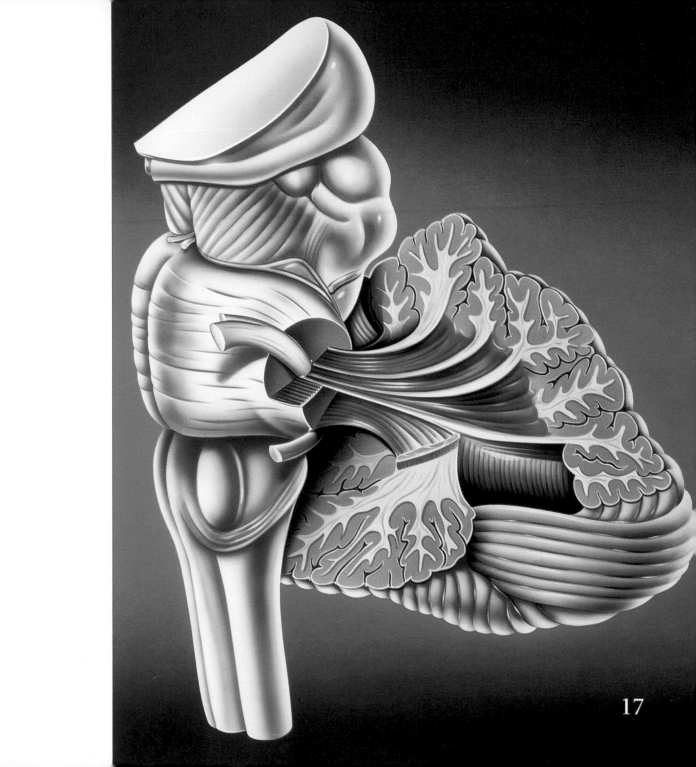

17

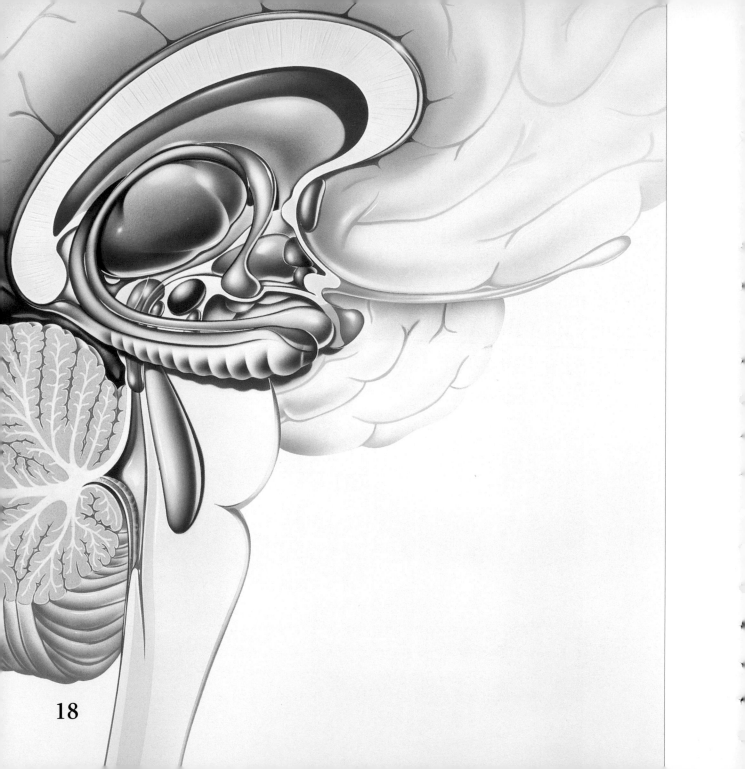

The Limbic System

You can think of the limbic system as the home of your emotions and moods. In the limbic system, several areas of the brain work together. It is here that you connect feelings with strong physical reactions—fear with a fast heartbeat, for instance. Emotions such as anger, fear, and joy are all organized in the limbic system. Your limbic system also influences how you form memories.

Deep within your brain lies the limbic system, nervous system tissue involved in instinct and mood. When you feel pleasure or anger, for instance, your limbic system may have helped your brain recognize those emotions.

Memories are storage places of information. Scientists think that, in order to create memories, nerve cells form new molecules and new connections. No single region of your brain stores all your memories because the storage site depends on the type of memory. For example, you hold information about riding a bike in the motor areas of your brain, while the auditory areas hold the words to your favorite song. Without memory, you could not learn anything, because as soon as you saw, heard, or felt something, you would forget it.

Different parts of your brain are responsible for different activities you perform. When you ride a bike, for instance, the motor areas of the brain work to make it possible.

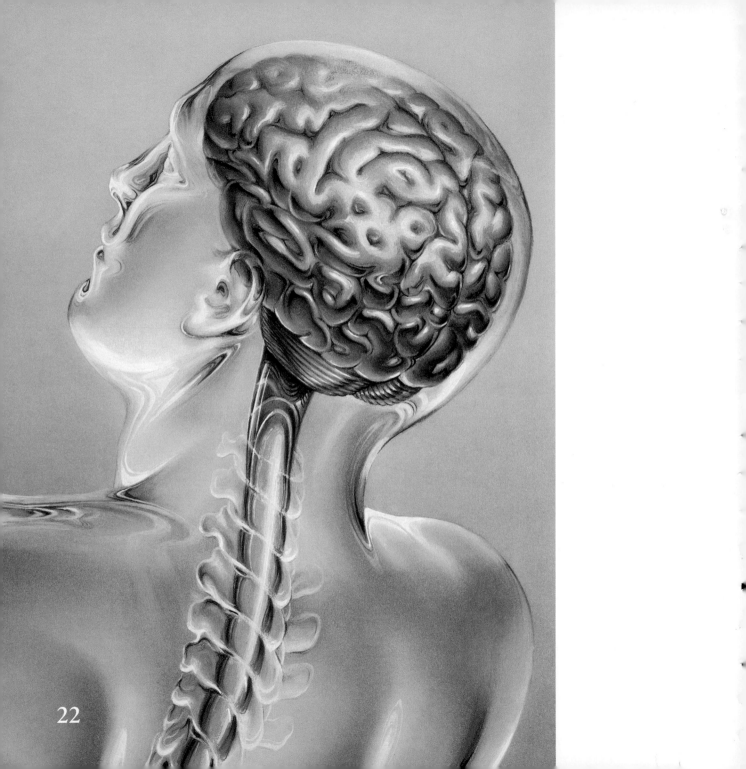

The Spinal Cord

Your brain, along with your spinal cord, make up the central nervous system. Reach around and feel the bones of your spine with your fingers. Those bony segments you feel form the spinal column, which protects the spinal cord. The spinal cord is a cable of nerve tissue that transmits messages to and from the brain and the rest of your body. In the average-sized adult, the spinal cord is about seventeen inches in length. It is about as wide as your finger. Thirty-one pairs of spinal nerves connect the spinal cord to the nerves in the rest of the body. The spinal nerves relay sensory information to the brain. They also carry signals from the brain to the muscles, telling them how to move.

The spinal cord is a column of nerve tissue that contains thirty-one pairs of spinal nerves. Bones called vertebrae protect these nerves.

YOU'VE GOT SOME NERVE

The nerves that branch out into every part of the body make up what is called your *peripheral nervous system*. Some peripheral nerves receive information from your skin, internal organs, and the outside world. These nerves are called *sensory nerves*. *Motor nerves* work to move your voluntary muscles. *Autonomic nerves* regulate the internal organs and glands to make sure your body maintains its internal harmony.

The peripheral nerves extend from the spinal cord to transmit information both to and from the brain.

When you exercise, sympathetic nerves tell your heart to work faster. But when you are resting, like the girls in this picture, parasympathetic nerves tell your heart to slow down.

There are two types of autonomic nerves. The *sympathetic nerves* excite the body, speeding up its processes in response to stimuli. The *parasympathetic nerves* bring the processes back to normal. When you run, your sympathetic nerves speed up your heart rate, tense your muscles, and get you breathing hard. When you relax your parasympathetic nerves return your heartbeat, level of muscle tension, and breathing back to normal.

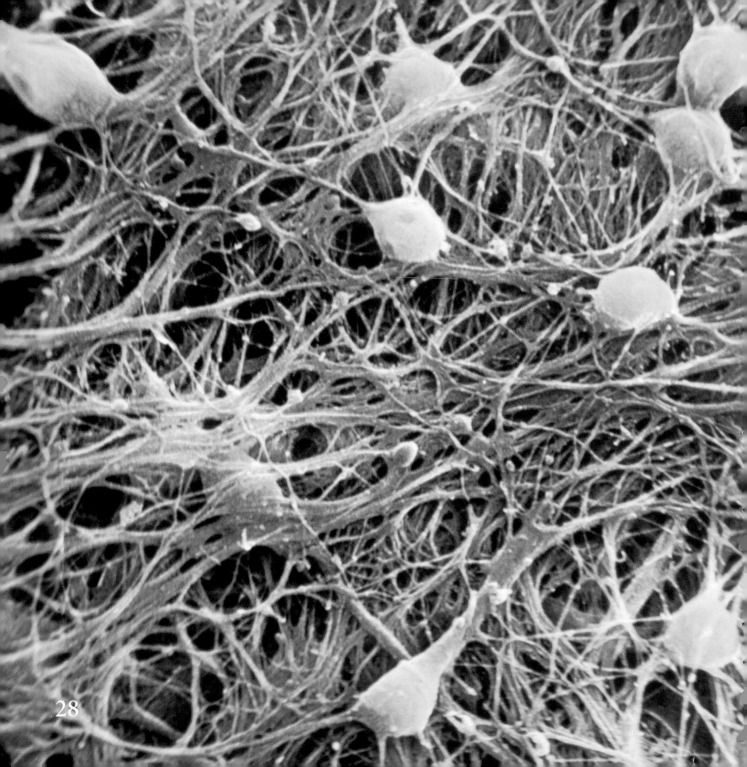

28

HOW NERVES WORK

The brain, spinal cord, and peripheral nerves are made up of neurons. Most neurons are so small, they can only be seen under a microscope. Each neuron contains three important parts: the central body, the dendrites, and the axon. Messages from other nerve cells enter the cell body through the dendrites, branchlike projections extending from the cell body. Once the central cell body processes the messages, it can pass on the information to the next nerve cell. It does this through a cablelike fiber called the axon.

Neurons are individual nerve cells, and billions of neurons connected together in bundles make up the nervous system.

However, there is a gap between the axon of one neuron and the dendrites of another. That gap is called a *synapse*. For a message to make it across this gap, it requires the help of certain chemicals, called *neurotransmitters*. Neurotransmitters are made in the cell body and stored in the axon of a nerve cell. When a cell is ready to send a message, its axon releases a certain type of neurotransmitter, which allows the message to pass into the next nerve cell. At speeds faster than you can imagine, information zips through your body from one neuron to another in just this way.

Tiny fibers called dendrites transmit messages from one neuron to another.

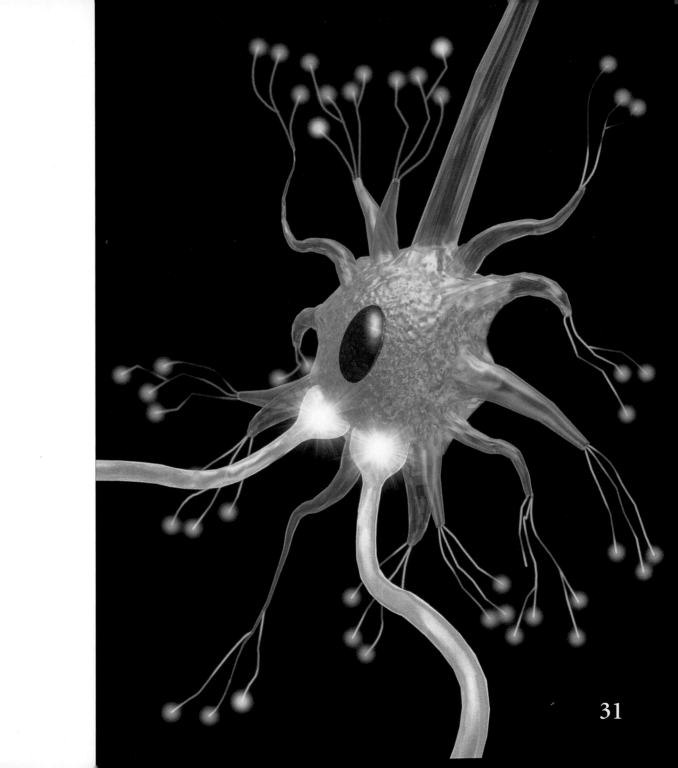

32

Information about everything—from movement to speech to what you see and taste—travel to and from your brain through the nervous system from all parts of the body.

WHEN THINGS GO WRONG

Most of the time, your brain and nervous system work just fine. However, there are some diseases, injuries, and common ailments that can cause problems.

Injuries

Severe blows or wounds to the head and spinal cord can affect the way the brain and nervous system work. A concussion occurs when the brain moves suddenly within the skull after a blow to the head. It causes a loss of consciousness, vomiting, and severe headache. A concussion rarely causes serious damage, but it does require immediate medical attention. Injury to the spinal cord can result in a loss of movement in the body called paralysis.

When injury or disease destroys certain nerve cells of the spinal cord, nerve signals can no longer travel to the legs, and this causes paralysis.

Headaches

Headaches are one of the most common problems, even among young people. The most common kind of headache occurs when the muscles of the head and neck tense up. This is called a *tension headache*. Learning to relax is one of the best ways to help this type of headache. Another kind of headache, called a *migraine,* results from blood vessels on the scalp, near the eye, or in the neck expanding and causing pressure. Doctors have several different medications that treat migraine.

This woman appears to have a tension headache, which occurs when the muscles of the head and neck become tense.

Epilepsy

About one in every one hundred people is affected by epilepsy. This disorder involves a disturbance of electrical signals in the brain, which alters consciousness and can cause involuntary movements called *seizures*. Often the cause of epilepsy is unknown. Doctors can help people with epilepsy control their disease with medication.

When nerve signal transmissions in the brain become disturbed, a condition known as epilepsy may exist.

Strokes

Strokes are a form of brain damage. They occur when something such as a blood clot interrupts the blood flow to the brain. Blood normally brings oxygen and nutrients to brain cells. If the brain lacks blood, then cells die. Strokes usually happen to older people who have heart disease or high blood pressure.

A person who suffers from a stroke—an injury to the brain caused by blood loss—may have to learn to write or speak all over again.

KEEP THINKING AND MOVING

There are no specific foods to eat or exercise routines to follow to keep your brain and nervous system healthy. But make sure you eat a balanced diet and get plenty of rest. You should also plan to exercise on a regular basis—not only your body, but also your mind. Research shows that the more you learn, the stronger your brain power will be throughout your life.

You should also take precautions to prevent a brain injury. Wear a helmet while riding your bike, in-line skating, or participating in contact sports. You should always wear a seat belt whenever you ride in a car. You want your brain to last you your whole life, so start now to keep it safe, healthy, and vital.

Always protect your brain by wearing a helmet when you skate or ride a bike and buckling your safety belt when you're riding in a car.

43

Autonomic nerves regulate body functions that you have little or no control over, like digestion and breathing

Axons fibers that extend from a nerve cell and carry messages away from the cell

Brain stem part of the brain that connects the major portions of the brain with the spinal cord

Cerebellum part of the brain that controls movement

Cerebrum the largest portion of the brain, it is responsible for thinking and voluntary movement

Central nervous system the brain and the spinal cord

Cerebral cortex the outer layer of the cerebrum, responsible for memory, intellect, and the senses

Cortex the outer layer of the cerebrum

Dendrites fibers that extend from nerve cells and receive information from other nerve cells

Limbic system the part of the brain that scientists believe is home to the emotions and the drive for self-preservation

Membranes thin layers of tissue that surround organs

Migrane headaches a type of headache that results from blood vessels on the scalp, near the eye, or in the neck expanding and causing pressure

Motor nerves   nerves that move your voluntary muscles

Neurotransmitters   chemicals in the brain and the body that help transmit messages to and from the nervous system and other parts of the body

Neurons   nerve cells

Parasympathetic nerves   the part of the nervous system that prepares the body for stress

Peripheral nervous system   the nerves that extend from the brain and spinal cord to the rest of the body's organs and tissues

Sensory nerves   nerves that receive information from your skin, internal organs, and the outside world

Stimulus   anything that causes the body to react in any way

Sympathetic nerves   the part of the nervous system that restores energy after the body reacts to stress

Synapse   the space between nerve cells over which messages about movement and other reactions must pass

tension headache   a type of headache caused when the muscles of the neck and head tense up

Voluntary muscles   muscles that does its work automatically, requiring no thought

FIND OUT MORE

BOOKS:

Clayman, Charles. *The Human Body: An Illustrated Guide to Its Structure, Function, and Disorders.* London: Dorling Kindersley Limited, 1995.

The Children's Book of the Body. Brookfield, CT: Copper Beech Books, 1996.

Farndon, John. *The Big Book of the Brain: All about the Body's Control Center.* Peter Bedrick Books, 2000.

Parker, Steve. *The Brain and Nerves.* Brookfield, CT: Copper Beech Books, 1998.

Treays, Rebecca. *Understanding Your Brain.* EDC Publications, 1996.

WEBSITES:

KidsHealth
http://kidshealth.org/kid/body/brain_SW.html

BrainPop
http://www.brainpop.com/health/nervous/brain/index.index.weml

AUTHOR'S BIO

Suzanne LeVert is a writer and editor of young adult and trade books with more than 30 titles to her credit. Although she specializes in health topics, Suzanne also enjoys writing about history and politics, and is the author of *Louisiana* and *Massachusetts* in the Benchmark Books series, *Celebrate the States.* Suzanne currently lives in New Orleans and attends Tulane Law School.

INDEX

Page numbers for illustrations are in boldface.

aging, 41, 42
autonomic nerves, 24-27, **26**, 44
axons, 29, 44

balance, 15
blood, 7-8, 41
brain
    appearance, 7, 11
    divisions, 8, **9**
brain stem, 16, **17**, 44
breathing, 16

cells, nerve. See neurons
central nervous system, 23, 44

cerebellum, 15, **16**, 44
cerebral cortex, 44
cerebrum, **10**, 11-12, 44
chemicals, 30
concussion, 34
coordination, 15
cortex, 12, 44

decision-making, 11
dendrites, 29, **31**, 44
digestion, 16

emotions, 19
energy, 7-8
epilepsy, 38, **39**

exercise, 27, 42

fear, 16, 19

glands, 24

headaches, **36**, 37
healthy practices, 42, **43**
heartbeat, 16, 27
hemispheres, **10**

internal organs, 24

learning, 11, 20, 42
limbic system, **18**, 19, 44

membranes, 7, 44
memories, 19-20
message transmission, 29-30, **31**, **32-33**, 38
migraine headaches, 37, 44-45
moods, 19
motor activity, 20, **21**
motor nerves, 24, 45
movement
    precise, 15
    voluntary, 12

neurons, **28**, 29, 45
neurotransmitters, 30, 45
nutrients, 7-8, 41

oxygen, 7-8, 16, 41

paralysis, 34, **35**
parasympathetic nerves, **26**, 27, 45
peripheral nervous system, 24, **25**, 45
protection, **6**, 7, 23, 42, **43**

seizures, 38
sensory nerves, 24, 45
skull, **6**
sneezing, 16
spinal cord, **22**, 23
stairs, walking down, 15
stimulus, 45
strokes, **40**, 41
swallowing, 16
sympathetic nerves, 27, 45
synapses, 30, 45

tension, **36**, 37
tension headaches, 45
thinking, 11

vertebrae, **22**, 23
voluntary muscles, 12, **13**, 24, 45

weight, 7